Laboratory Ma

CONCEPTS AND CH

EARTH AND SPACE

Martin Schachter ◆ Alan Winkler ◆ Stanley Wolfe

Stanley Wolfe
Project Coordinator

GLOBE FEARON
Pearson Learning Group

The following people have contributed to the development of this product:

Art and Design: Evelyn Bauer, Susan Brorein, Tracey Gerber, Bernadette Hruby, Carol Marie Kiernan, Mindy Klarman, Judy Mahoney, Karen Mancinelli, Elbaliz Mendez, April Okano, Dan Thomas, Jennifer Visco

Editorial: Stephanie P. Cahill, Gina Dalessio, Nija Dixon, Martha Feehan, Theresa McCarthy, Maurice Sabean, Marilyn Sarch, Maury Solomon, S. Adrienn Vegh-Soti, Shirley C. White, Jeffrey Wickersty

Manufacturing: Mark Cirillo, Tom Dunne

Marketing: Maureen Christensen, Douglas Falk

Production: Irene Belinsky, Linda Bierniak, Carlos Blas, Karen Edmonds, Cheryl Golding, Leslie Greenberg, Roxanne Knoll, Susan Levine, Cynthia Lynch, Jennifer Murphy, Lisa Svoronos, Susan Tamm

Publishing Operations: Carolyn Coyle, Thomas Daning, Richetta Lobban

Technology: Jessie Lin, Joanne Saito, Ellen Strain

About the Cover: Our Sun is one of about 100 billion stars in the Milky Way Galaxy, part of which is shown in the larger photograph. Orbiting the Sun are nine planets, including Earth. The smaller photograph shows Earth as seen from space, where it appears to be rising above its only natural satellite, the Moon.

ISBN: 0-13-024229-2

Printed in the United States of America

1 2 3 4 5 6 7 8 9 10   07 06 05 04 03

Globe Fearon
Pearson Learning Group

1-800-321-3106
www.pearsonlearning.com

CONTENTS

Notes

SAFETY IN THE SCIENCE LABORATORY

Unlike many other fields of study, science allows you an opportunity to "learn by doing." Part of this process often involves work both in the laboratory and in the field.

Working a science laboratory can be both exciting and meaningful. However, when carrying out experiments, you may sometimes work with materials that can be dangerous if not handled properly. For this reason, you must always be aware of proper safety procedures. You can avoid accidents in the laboratory by following a few simple guidelines:

- **Always** handle all material carefully.
- **Never** perform a laboratory investigation without direction from your teacher.
- **Never** work alone in the science laboratory.
- **Always** read directions in a laboratory investigation before beginning the laboratory.

Throughout this laboratory program, you will see the safety symbols that are shown below and on the next page. Before beginning any laboratory, be sure to read the laboratory and note any safety symbols and caution statements. If you know what each symbol means, and always follow the guidelines that apply to each symbol, your work in the laboratory will be both safe and exciting.

SAFETY SYMBOLS

Clothing Protection
- Wear your laboratory apron to protect your clothing from stains or burns.

Eye Safety
- Wear your laboratory goggles, especially when working with open flames and chemicals.
- If chemicals get into your eyes, flush your eyes with plenty of water. Notify your teacher immediately.
- Be sure you know how to use the emergency eyewash system in the laboratory.

Clean Up
- Always wash your hands after an activity in which you handle chemicals, animals, or plants.

Disposal
- Keep your work area clean at all times.
- Dispose of all materials properly. Follow your teacher's instructions for disposal.

Glassware Safety
- Handle glassware carefully.
- Check all glassware for chips or cracks before using it. Never use glassware that has chips or cracks.
- Do not try to clean up broken glassware. Notify your teacher if you break a piece of glassware.
- Air dry all glassware. Do not use paper towels to dry glassware.
- Never force glass tubing into the hole of a rubber stopper.

Heating Safety
- Be careful when handling hot objects.
- Turn off the hot plate or other heat source when you are not using it.
- When you heat chemicals in a test tube, always point the test tube away from people.

Fire Safety

- Confine loose clothing and tie back long hair when working near an open flame.
- Be sure you know the location of fire extinguishers and fire blankets in the laboratory.
- Never reach across an open flame.

Dangerous Chemicals

- Use extreme care when working with acids and bases. Both acids and bases can cause burns. If you spill an acid or a base on your skin, flush your skin with plenty of water. Notify your teacher immediately.
- Never mix chemicals unless you are instructed to do so by your teacher.
- Never pour water into an acid or a base. Always pour an acid or a base into water.
- Never smell anything directly.
- Use caution when handling chemicals that produce fumes.

Poison

- Never use chemicals without directions from your teacher.
- Use all poisonous chemicals with extreme caution.
- Inform your teacher immediately if you spill chemicals or get any chemicals in your eyes or on your skin.

Sharp Objects

- Be careful when using scissors, scalpels, knives, or other cutting instruments.
- Always dissect specimens in a dissecting pan. Never dissect a specimen while holding it in your hand.
- Always cut in the direction away from your body.

Electrical Safety

- Check electrical equipment for loose plugs or worn cords before using it.
- Be sure that electrical cords are not placed where people can trip over them.
- Do not use electrical equipment with wet hands or near water.
- Never overload an electrical circuit.

Plant Safety

- Never eat any part of a plant that you cannot identify as edible.
- Some plants, such as poison ivy, are harmful if they are touched or eaten. Use caution when handling or collecting plants. Always use a reliable field guide to plants.

Animal Safety

- Be careful when handling live animals. Some animals can injure you or spread disease.
- Do not bring live animals into class that have not been purchased from a reputable pet store.

⚠ Caution

- Follow the ⚠ CAUTION and safety symbols you see used throughout this manual when doing labs or other activities.

SCIENCE EQUIPMENT AND APPARATUS

As you work in the science laboratory, you will need to become familiar with many pieces of equipment and apparatus. Several common pieces of equipment are shown below and on the next page. Below the name of each piece of equipment is a brief description of what the equipment is used for.

Metric ruler
Used to measure length

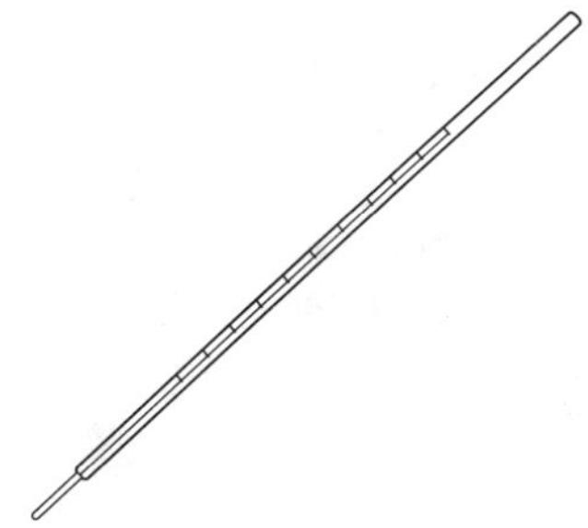

Thermometer
Used to measure temperature in degrees Celsius

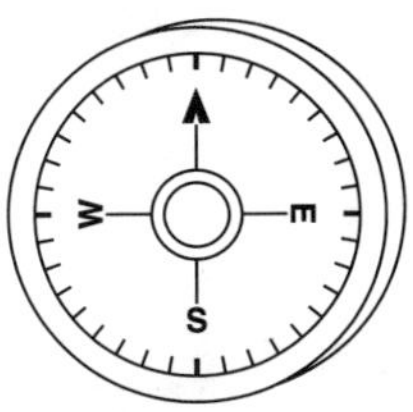

Compass
Used to determine direction

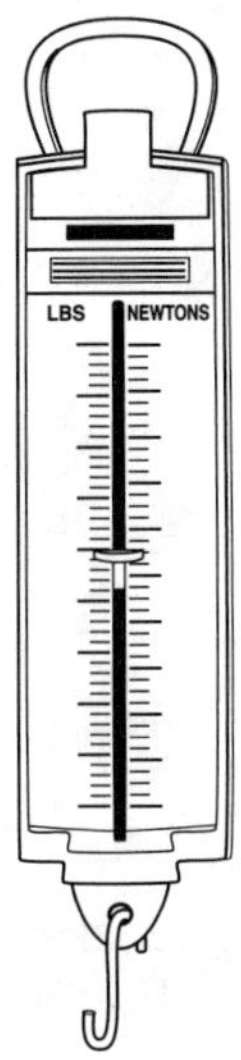

Spring scale
Used to measure weight

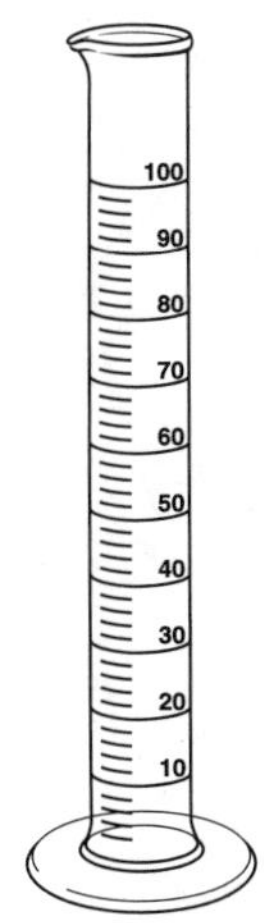

Graduated cylinder
Used to measure volume

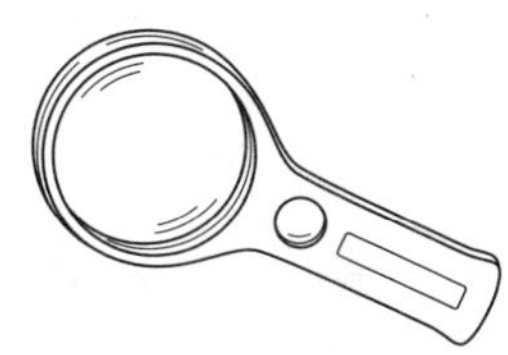

Hand lens
Used to make things appear larger

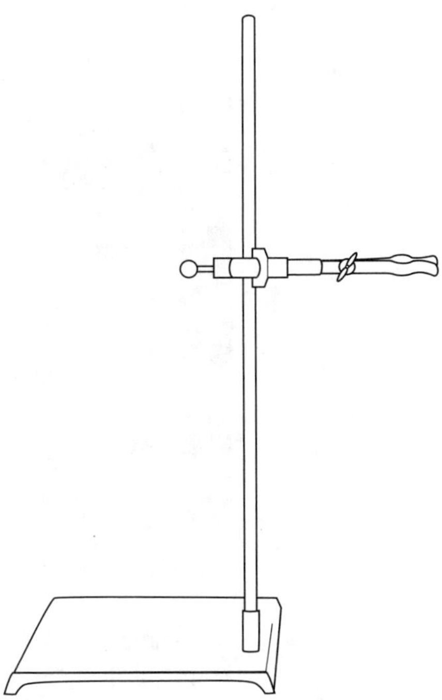

Ring stand with clamp
Used to hold equipment steady

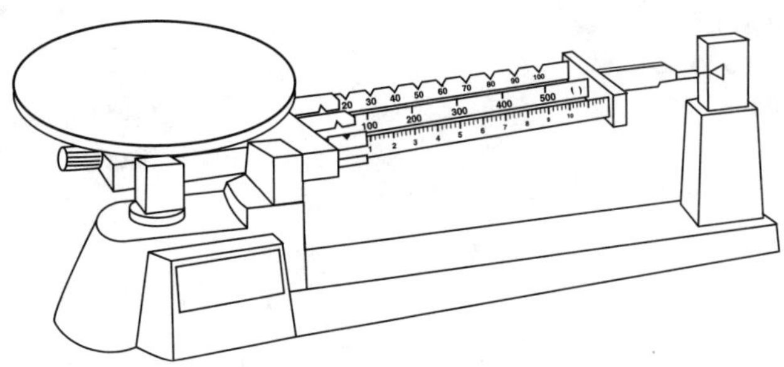

Triple-beam balance
Used to measure mass

SCIENCE EQUIPMENT AND APPARATUS

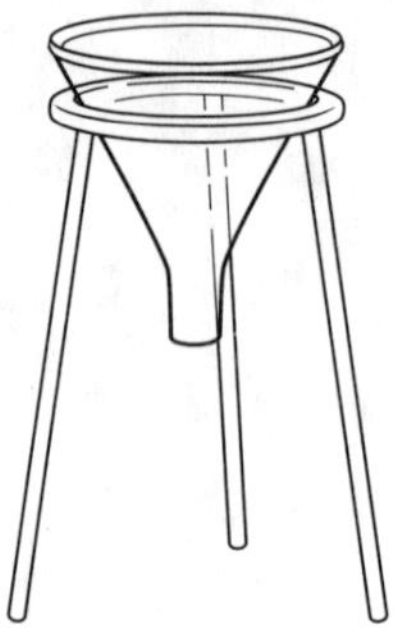

Funnel and tripod
Used to hold materials through which water trickles

Dropper
Used to add small amounts of liquids

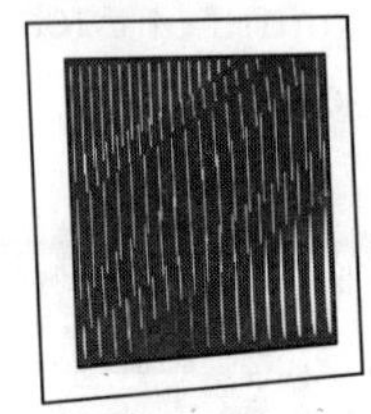

Diffraction grating
Used to separate light

Stirring rod
Used to mix materials

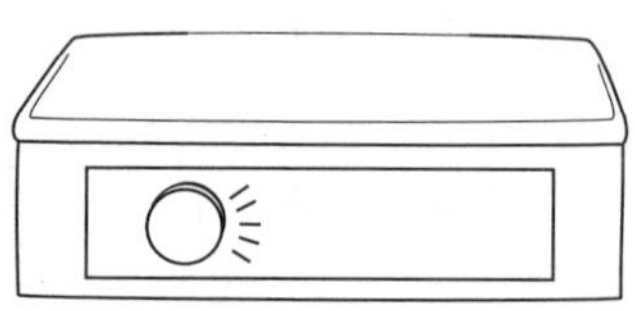

Hot plate
Used to heat materials

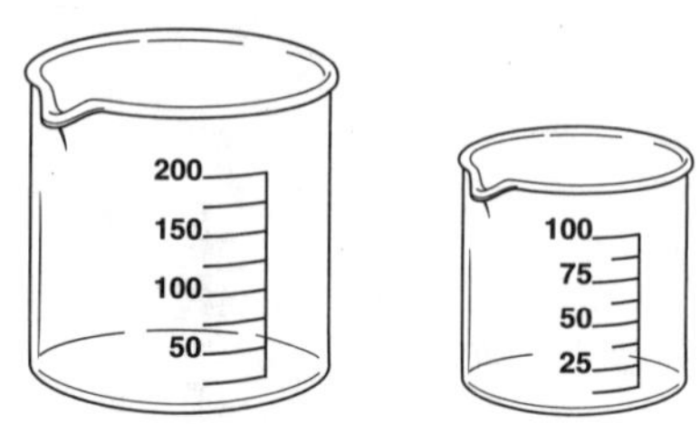

Beakers
Used to hold materials

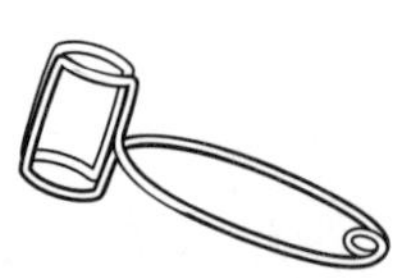

Test tube holder
Used to hold hot test tubes

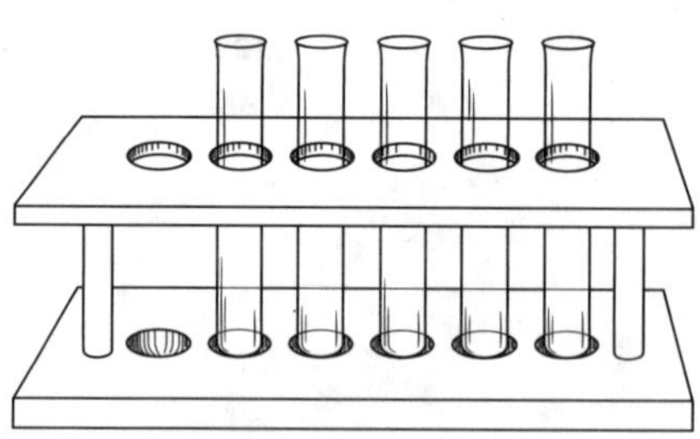

Test tubes and rack
Used to hold materials

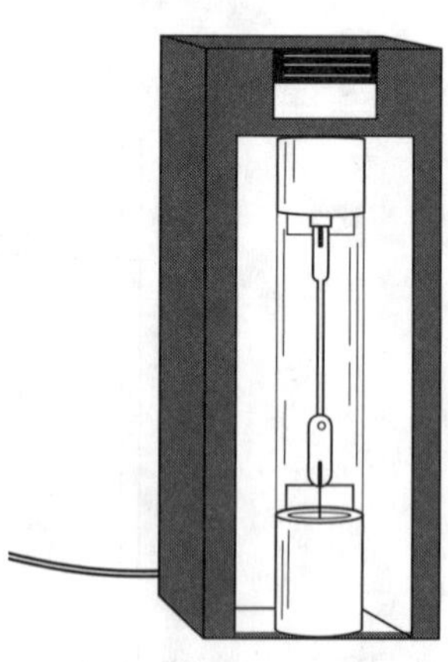

Gas vapor tube
Used to produce a spectrum for certain elements

Name ______________________ Class ______________ Date ______________

LABORATORY SKILLS WORKSHEET 1

Using a Graduated Cylinder

Materials

100-mL graduated cylinder
dropper
small jar

BACKGROUND: A graduated cylinder is used to measure the volume of a liquid. A graduated cylinder is a long tube marked along its side with lines that show the volume. Some graduated cylinders are small and measure only up to 10 milliliters of liquid. Others are larger and measure 25 milliliters, 100 milliliters, or more. Notice the 10-milliliter graduated cylinder in Figure 1. The long lines below the numbers show milliliters. The shorter lines show two-tenths of a milliliter. Other graduated cylinders may have different values for the long and short lines. When you pour a liquid into a graduated cylinder, you can use these lines to determine the volume of the liquid.

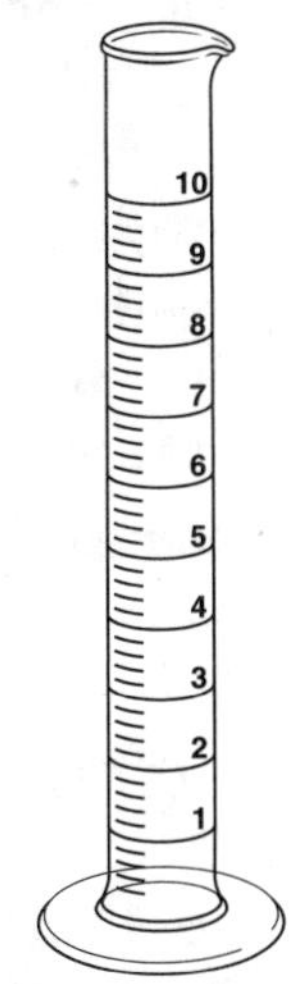

▲ **Figure 1** A 10-mL graduated cylinder

PURPOSE: In this activity, you will learn how to use a graduated cylinder.

PROCEDURE

Part A: Reading a Graduated Cylinder

❑ 1. **OBSERVE:** Look at a graduated cylinder. Notice the markings on the side. The markings on a graduated cylinder are usually given in milliliters, which is abbreviated mL. Record information about this graduated cylinder in Table 1 on page 6.

❑ 2. Look at the graduated cylinder shown in Figure 2. Notice that the surface of the liquid is curved upward at the sides. This curve is called a meniscus. When you read the volume of a liquid in a graduated cylinder, you must look at it from eye level. Always read the volume at the flat, center part of the meniscus. In Figure 2, the volume is 8.6 mL.

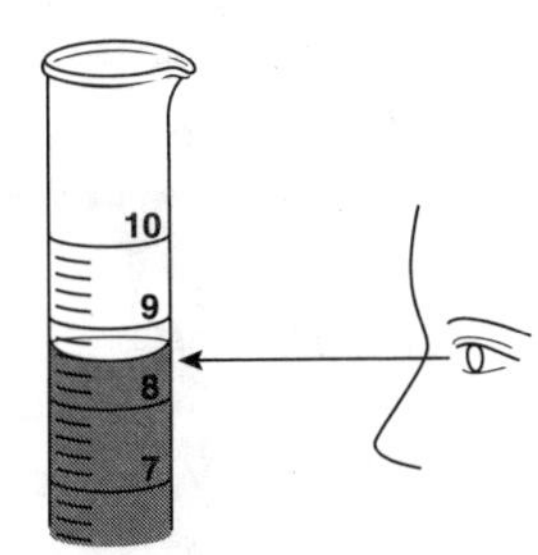

▲ **Figure 2** Reading the meniscus of a liquid in a graduated cylinder

❑ 3. Look at the graduated cylinder readings in Figure 3. Write the volume of the liquid in each graduated cylinder in the space provided.

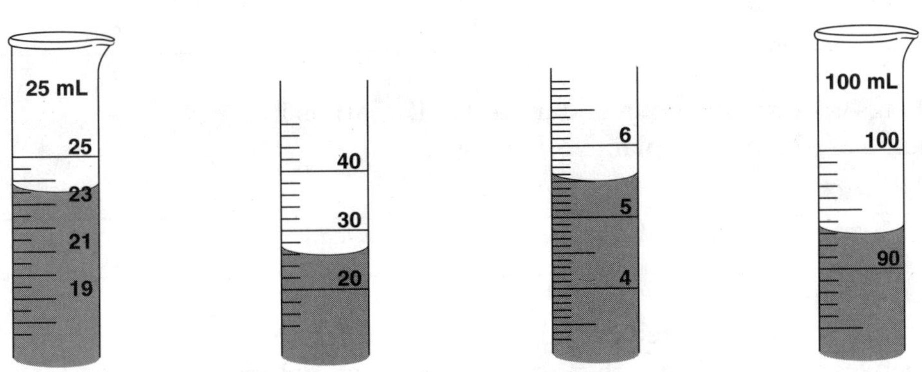

1. ____________ 2. ____________ 3. ____________ 4. ____________

▲ **Figure 3** Write the volume of liquid in each graduated cylinder.

Part B: Measuring the Volume of a Liquid

❑ 1. **MEASURE:** Half fill a small jar with water. Pour the water into the graduated cylinder. Record the volume of the water in Table 2. Ask your teacher to check your answer. Empty your graduated cylinder.

❑ 2. Repeat Step 4 two more times. Have your lab partner check your answers.

❑ 3. **MEASURE:** Use a graduated cylinder to measure 64 mL of water. First, fill the jar with water. Pour water from the jar into the graduated cylinder until it is between the 60 and 70-mL mark. Look at the meniscus from eye level. If the reading is greater than 64 mL, pour some of the water back into the jar. If the reading is less than 64 mL, use a dropper to get water from the jar and add it to the graduated cylinder. Continue until the lower part of the meniscus is on the 64-mL line.

❑ 4. Repeat Step 3 to measure 82 mL and 93 mL. Have your lab partner check your readings each time.

OBSERVATIONS

Table 1: Information About the Graduated Cylinder	
Greatest volume it will measure	
Volume shown by the longest lines	
Volume shown by the shortest lines	

Table 2: Reading a Graduated Cylinder	
Volume 1	
Volume 2	
Volume 3	

CONCLUSIONS

1. **COMPARE:** What is an advantage of measuring a liquid with a graduated cylinder instead of a beaker? ______________________________

____

2. **INFER:** If the smallest markings on a graduated cylinder are 1 mL apart, is it possible to measure a volume of 63.5 mL? Explain your answer.

____

____

3. Suppose that the long markings on a graduated cylinder are 1 mL apart and there are four short lines between the 8-mL and the 9-mL marks. What volumes do the short lines indicate?

____

____

Name ______________________ Class ______________ Date ______________

LABORATORY SKILLS WORKSHEET 2

Using a Triple-Beam Balance

Materials

- solid object
- 150-mL beaker
- salt
- tablespoon
- triple-beam balance

BACKGROUND: Triple-beam balances are often used to find the mass of solid objects or powdered solids. Most triple-beam balances have a balance pan, three beams, a pointer, and a three-part scale with riders. Many balances also have an adjustment knob. The scale of a balance measures grams. The scale of the top beam gives readings in 10-gram intervals, for example, 10 grams, 20 grams, and so on, up to 100 grams. The scale of the middle beam gives readings in hundreds of grams. The scale of the bottom beam gives readings in grams from 1 gram to 10 grams. Each 1-gram interval shows tenths of a gram, from 0.1 gram to 0.9 gram. A triple-beam balance measures the mass of an object by balancing the mass in the pan with the riders on the scale.

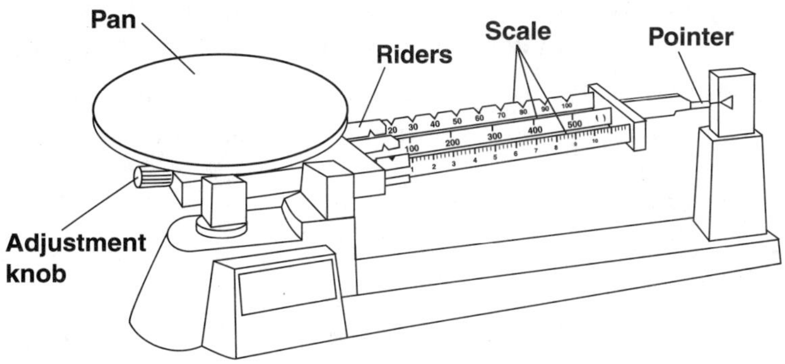

PURPOSE: In this activity, you will learn how to use a triple-beam balance.

PROCEDURE

Part A: Reading a Mass

❑ **1.** To read the mass of an object, read the position of the hundreds, tens, and ones riders to find the mass in hundreds, tens, ones, and tenths of grams. Read the mass shown on the triple-beam balance scale below.

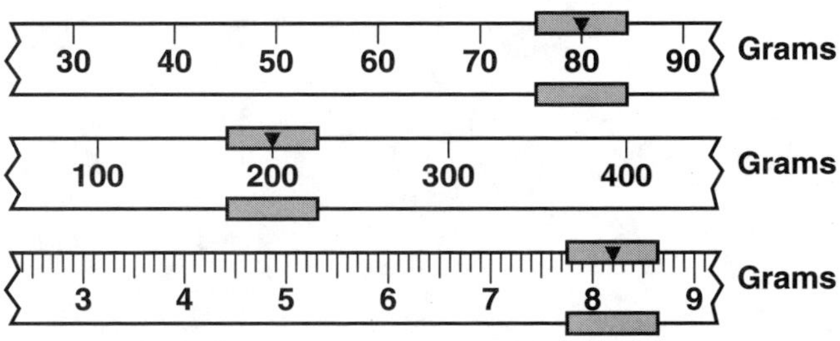

Table 1: Reading a Mass	
Rider	**Mass**
Tens rider	
Hundreds rider	
Ones rider	
Total mass	

❑ **2. RECORD:** Record the mass shown by each rider in Table 1. Make sure that you write a decimal point before the number of tenths shown on the ones rider.

❑ **3.** Add the masses together to find the total mass. Record this in Table 1.

Part B: Finding the Mass of a Solid Object

❑ **1.** Before using a triple-beam balance, make sure that the balance is centered properly. Set all the riders to zero. The balance pointer should rest at the zero mark at the end of the scale. If the balance pointer is not at zero, turn the adjustment knob until the pointer arrives at zero.

- ❑ **2.** Place the object on the balance pan.
- ❑ **3. MEASURE:** Slide the riders until the pointer is once again on zero. This means that the scale is balanced. If the mass of the object is less than 10 grams, you will find that you do not need to move the top rider. If the mass of the object is less than 100 grams, you will not need to move the middle rider.
- ❑ **4. RECORD:** To find the mass of the object, first record the measurement shown on each of the three riders. Record this information in Table 2. Then, add the masses of each rider to find the total mass. Record your measurement in Table 2.

Part C: Finding the Mass of a Substance

- ❑ **1. MODEL:** Place a beaker on the balance pan to find its mass. Record this mass in Table 3.
- ❑ **2. MEASURE:** Place 1 tablespoon of salt in the beaker. Find the mass of the beaker and the salt combined. Record the mass in Table 3.
- ❑ **3. CALCULATE:** To find the mass of the salt alone, subtract the mass of the beaker from the combined mass of the beaker and salt. Record the mass of the salt in Table 3.

OBSERVATIONS

Table 2: Reading a Mass

Rider	Mass
Tens rider	
Hundreds rider	
Ones rider	
Total mass	

Table 3: Finding the Mass of a Substance

Mass of beaker (a)	
Mass of beaker plus salt (b)	
Total mass (b minus a)	

CONCLUSIONS

1. CALCULATE: What is the greatest mass that most triple-beam balances can accurately measure? ______________________________

2. INFER: If only the ones rider needs to be moved from zero to balance a mass on the balance pan, what is the largest mass that the object can have? ______________________________

3. INFER: If the hundreds rider is left at zero and the tens and ones riders are moved to balance the scale, what is the largest mass that the object in the balance pan can have?

____

Name ______________________ Class ______________ Date ______________

LABORATORY SKILLS WORKSHEET 3

Graphing

Materials

colored pencils

BACKGROUND: Graphs are a useful way to organize and present information. Graphing data helps you see similarities and patterns. It also helps other people understand your data. Four types of graphs that you can use are line graphs, bar graphs, circle graphs, and pictographs.

PURPOSE: In this activity, you will learn how to make different kinds of graphs.

PROCEDURE

Part A: Making a Line Graph

❑ 1. **OBSERVE:** Look at the line graph in Figure 1. Notice that data are plotted as points connected by a line. The horizontal axis shows the range of the independent variable. The vertical axis shows the range of the dependent variable. When graphing, you must decide which values are independent and which are dependent. In Figure 1, the mean temperature depends on the month. Therefore, the mean temperature is the dependent variable, which goes on the vertical axis. The month, the independent variable, is on the horizontal axis.

Monthly Mean Temperature of Seattle, Washington

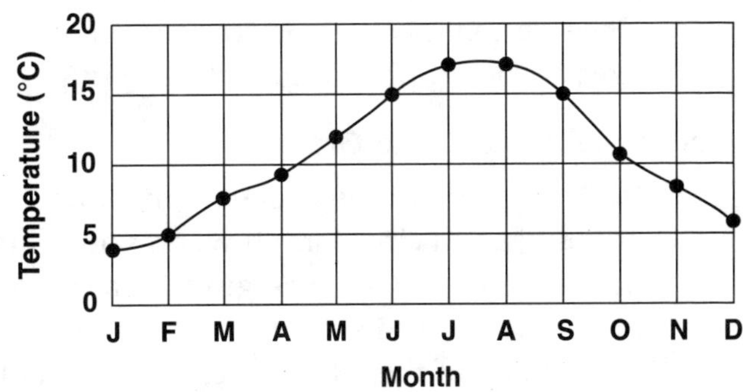

▲ **Figure 1** Line graph

❑ 2. **GRAPH:** Use the following information and data in Table 1 to create a line graph in the Observations section on page 11.

When meteorologists measure atmospheric pressure, they use a unit called the millibar (mb). Standard air pressure at sea level is 1,013 millibars. The figures in Table 1 describe how air pressure varies with altitude, or height above sea level.

Think about which variable is independent and which is dependent. Remember to include a title and to label the axes. Notice that the lowest air pressure is 3 mb and the highest is 1,013 mb. The air pressure range on your graph should be from 0 mb to just above 1,013 mb.

Table 1: Pressure Changes With Altitude

Altitude (km)	Air Pressure (mb)
0	1,013
1.0	899
2.0	795
3.0	701
4.0	617
5.0	540
10.0	265
20.0	55
30.0	12
40.0	3

Part B: Making a Bar Graph

❑ **1. OBSERVE:** Figure 2 shows a bar graph using the same data as in Figure 1. A bar graph is similar to a line graph except bars rather than points show the data. The bar graph in Figure 2 has the dependent variable on the vertical axis. Bar graphs may also be drawn so that the dependent variable is on the horizontal axis.

❑ **2. GRAPH:** Use the information in Table 1 on page 9 to create a bar graph in the Observations section. Be sure to label the axes of the graph and to include a title.

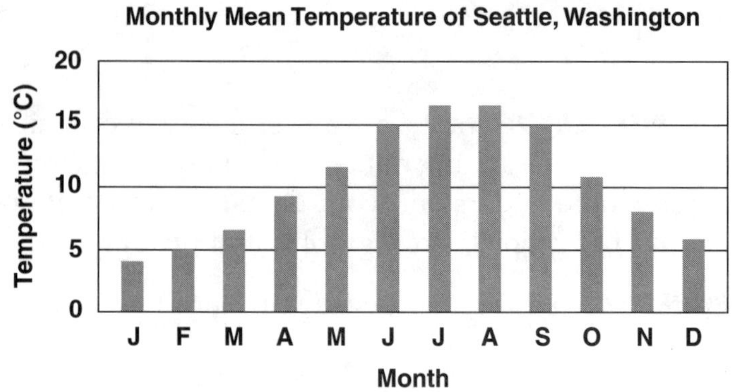

▲ **Figure 2** Bar graph

Part C: Making a Circle Graph

❑ **1. OBSERVE:** Look at the circle graph shown in Figure 3. You can use a circle graph when your data describe parts of a whole. A circle graph is a circle that is divided into sections. The size of each section shows a percentage of the whole circle. Notice that if you add the percentages of the sections together, they equal 100 percent.

❑ **2.** If the data are simple, you can draw a circle graph based on simple fractions of a whole. Suppose you want to graph the fractions of rock types you collected on a field trip: 5 limestone, 10 granite, and 5 sandstone. Since 5 is 1/4 of the total number of rocks, and 10 is 1/2 of the total number of rocks, your graph should look like Figure 4.

❑ **3. GRAPH:** In the Observations section on page 11, draw a circle graph showing the kinds of fossils found at a dig site. Assume that there are 12 fossils found: 6 saber-toothed cats, 4 giant sloths, and 2 woolly mammoths. Fill in the three sections, using colored pencils to make the graph easier to read. Label the sections and write a title for the graph.

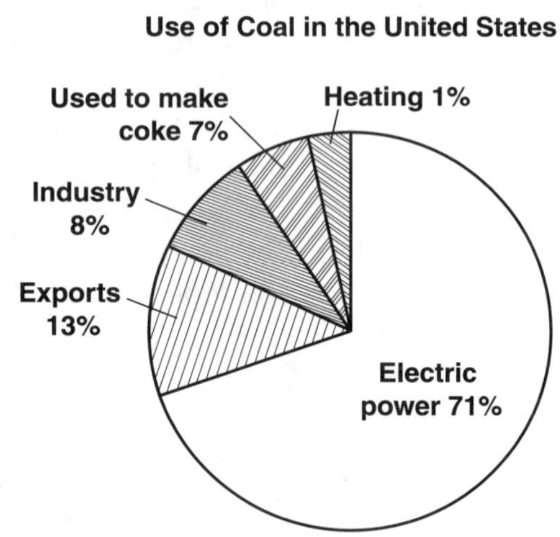

▲ **Figure 3** Circle graph using percentages

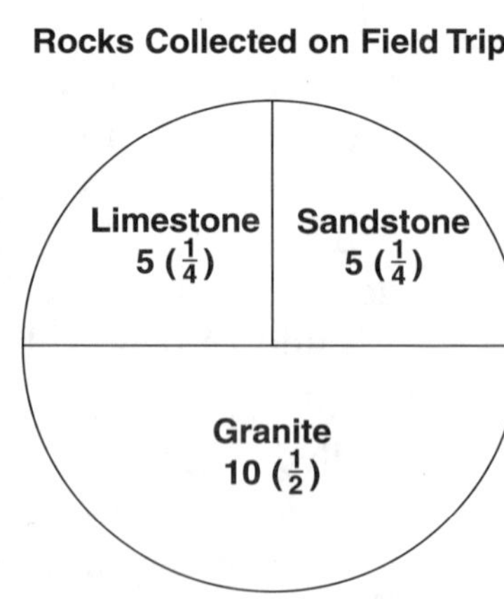

▲ **Figure 4** Circle graph using fractions

Part D: Making a Pictograph

❑ **1. OBSERVE:** As the name suggests, a pictograph is a graph using pictures. Look at the pictograph in Figure 5 on page 11. The uses of coal in the United States are represented by the amount of space they occupy on the picture. Figure 6 shows another type of pictograph. In this graph, small pictures represent fossils.

❑ **2. GRAPH:** Make a pictograph in the Observations section showing types of rocks found in a student's collection. Use the following data for your graph: 2 obsidian, 3 sandstone, 10 quartz, 2 marble, 6 coquina, 5 mica, 3 slate.

Name ______________________ Class ______________ Date ______________

LABORATORY SKILLS WORKSHEET 3 *(continued)*

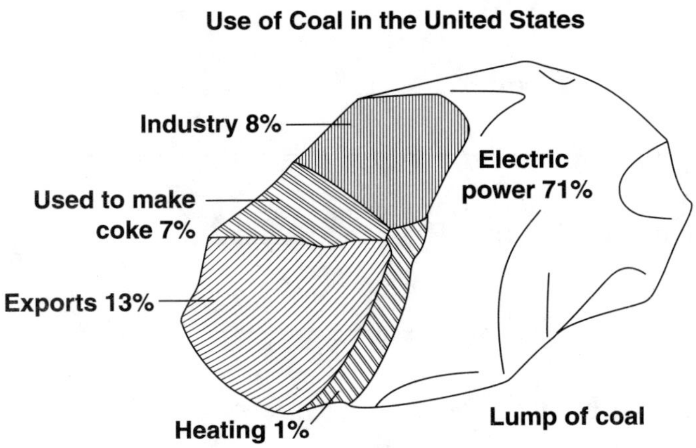

▲ **Figure 5** Pictograph showing percentages

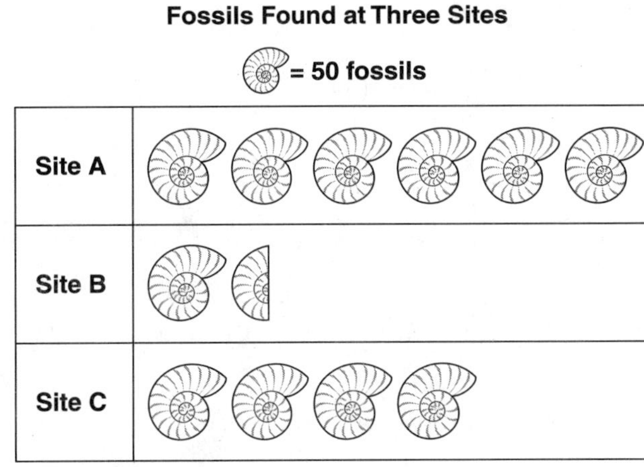

▲ **Figure 6** Pictograph based on numbers

OBSERVATIONS

▲ **Line Graph**

▲ **Bar Graph**

▲ **Circle Graph**

▲ **Pictograph**

CONCLUSIONS

1. What information is presented in the line graph shown in Figure 1? ______

______

2. What information is presented along the horizontal axis of Figure 1? ______

3. What information is presented along the vertical axis of Figure 2? ______

4. What is the independent variable in Figure 2? What is the dependent variable in Figure 2? ______

5. Look at the line graph in Figure 1. What trend do you see in the mean monthly temperature in Seattle? ______

6. How does the bar graph in Figure 2 show this same trend? ______

______

7. How would the bar graph shown in Figure 2 look different if the independent variable was on the vertical axis instead of on the horizontal axis?

______

8. Use the line graph in Figure 1 to determine the mean monthly temperature in Seattle in March. ______

9. What information is shown in the circle graph in Figure 3? ______

10. According to Figure 3, how is most of the coal in the United States used? What percentage of the total use is this amount? ______

11. According to Figure 3, what is the combined percentage of coal used in the United States for heating, industry, and electric power? ______

12. How does a pictograph make data easier to understand compared to using only numbers? ______

______

Name ________________ Class ________ Date ________

LABORATORY SKILLS WORKSHEET 4

Writing a Laboratory Report

Materials

pencil

BACKGROUND: When you perform a laboratory investigation, it is important to keep an organized record of what you do. It is also important to keep an accurate record of your results. An organized record of an investigation is called a laboratory report. A laboratory report is made up of the following sections: Title, Purpose, Background, Hypothesis, Materials, Procedure, Observations, Data, Analysis of Data, and Conclusions.

PURPOSE: In this activity, you will learn how to write a laboratory report.

PROCEDURE

❑ **1.** Study the following descriptions of the sections of a laboratory report.

Title—tells about the experiment
Purpose—reason for doing the experiment
Background—information that will help a reader understand the experiment better
Hypothesis—your idea on what you expect the results of the experiment to be
Materials—list of things needed to perform the experiment
Procedure—steps that will be followed during the experiment
Observations—description of what is seen during the experiment
Data—measurements made during the experiment
Analysis of Data—presentation of the data in tables, charts, graphs, or drawings
Conclusions—summary statement of the results; describes whether the data supported the hypothesis and sources of any errors

A group of students wanted to investigate the porosity of soils, or how easily water soaked through different kinds of soil. They suspected that water would travel through the soils at different rates. In order to test their idea, they constructed four identical setups of empty plastic milk bottles with the tops and bottoms cut off. Each bottle was placed on top of a bucket covered with plastic screening. Each bottle was half filled with one of the types of soil: Bottle A = gravel, Bottle B = sand, Bottle C = peat, Bottle D = clay.

Water from a container was poured through each soil type for a period of 1 minute and collected in the buckets. The students then measured the water from each bucket in a graduated cylinder. They observed that, in 1 minute, 100 mL of water traveled through the gravel; 70 mL through the sand; 30 mL through the peat; and 0 mL through the clay. Based on their results, the students decided that the porosity of the four different soils varies, with gravel having the highest porosity and clay the lowest.

❑ **2.** Reread the experiment described above. Write a possible title for the experiment.

____

❑ **3.** Notice the data that the students obtained in the experiment. Make a table to record data for the experiment in the Observations section on page 14.

OBSERVATIONS

CONCLUSIONS

1. State the purpose of this experiment in the form of a question. ______________________

____

2. What was the hypothesis in this experiment? ______________________

____

3. Make a list of materials that the students needed to carry out this experiment.

____

____

4. What variable was being tested in this experiment? ______________________

____

____

5. Write a step-by-step procedure for this experiment. ______________________

____

____

____

6. Write the conclusion that students reached based on their results. ______________________

____

Name ______________________ Class ______________ Date ______________

LABORATORY CHALLENGE FOR LESSON 1-4

How can you track the Sun's movement across the sky?

Materials

- atlas or almanac
- piece of heavy white paper (30 cm × 20 cm)
- piece of cardboard (40 cm × 40 cm)
- drawing compass
- protractor
- ruler or straightedge
- masking tape
- modeling clay
- plastic drinking straw
- magnetic compass

BACKGROUND: Every day, the Sun seems to rise in the east, travel across the sky, and set in the west. This apparent motion of the Sun is caused by Earth's rotation. Since the beginning of time, people have used these motions to mark the passage of time. One device used for this purpose is a sundial.

PURPOSE: In this activity, you will make a simple sundial that will allow you to make a record of the Sun's changing position in the daytime sky.

PROCEDURE

❑ **1. LOCATE:** Use an atlas or almanac to find the latitude of your community to the nearest 5°. You will use this information to make your sundial.

❑ **2.** Using a drawing compass, draw a semicircle with a diameter of 20 cm on a piece of heavy white paper, as shown in Figure 1. ⚠ **CAUTION: Be careful when using the compass. The point on which the compass turns is very sharp.**

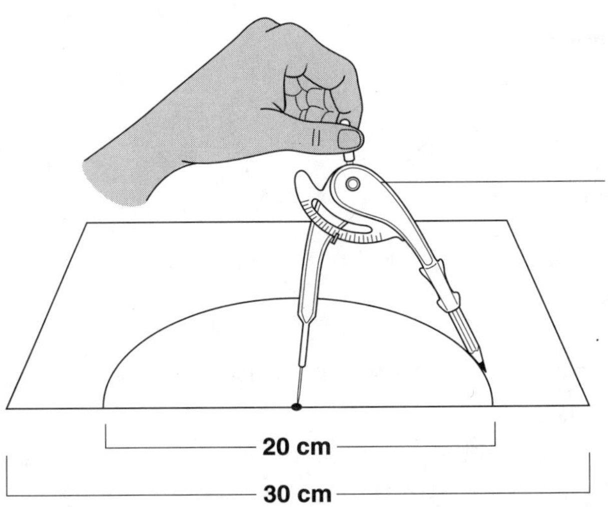

▲ **Figure 1** Draw a semicircle with a diameter of 20 cm.

❑ **3. MEASURE:** Place a protractor on the diameter of the semicircle and measure angles at 30° intervals, starting at 0° and ending at 180°. Use tic marks to indicate each angle, as shown in Figure 2 on page 16.

❑ **4.** Using a ruler or other straightedge, draw lines from the center of the diameter through each tic mark to the edge of the semicircle.

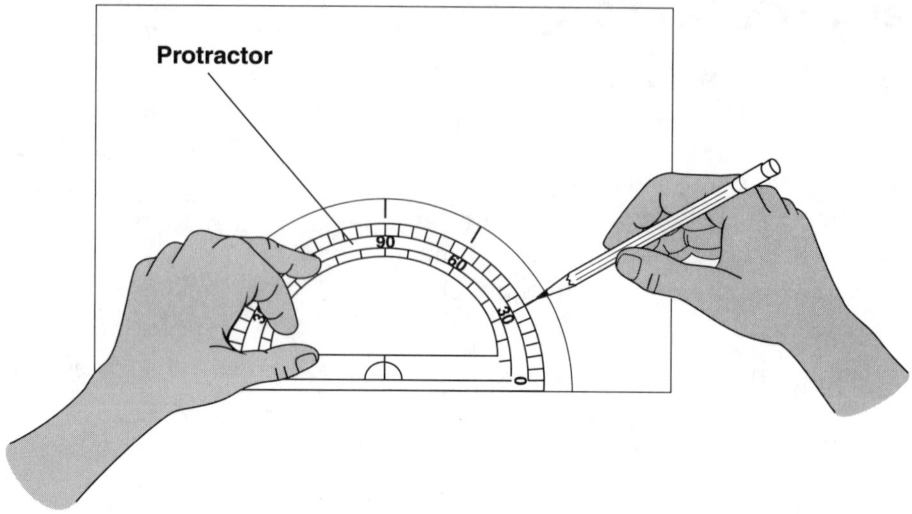

▲ **Figure 2** Measure angles at 30° intervals.

- ❑ **5.** Use masking tape to attach the white paper to a larger piece of cardboard.
- ❑ **6.** Place a small lump of modeling clay at the center of the diameter of the semicircle. Insert a plastic drinking straw into the clay. Tilt the straw so that the top of the straw is leaning toward the circumference of the semicircle, as shown in Figure 3.

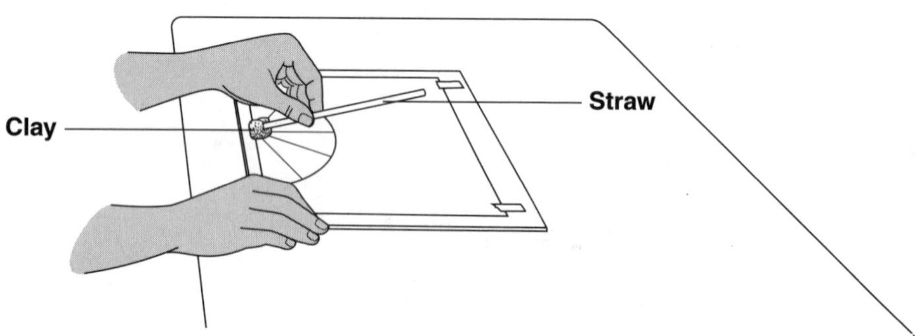

▲ **Figure 3** Tilt the straw toward the circumference of the semicircle.

- ❑ **7.** Using the protractor, adjust the angle of the straw's tilt to match the latitude of your community, as shown in Figure 4 on page 17.
- ❑ **8.** Carefully carry your sundial to a location where it can be placed in direct sunlight all day. Using a magnetic compass, arrange the sundial so that the straw lines up in a north-south direction, with the elevated tip of the straw pointing north.

Name ______________________ Class ______________ Date ______________

LABORATORY CHALLENGE FOR LESSON 1-4 *(continued)*

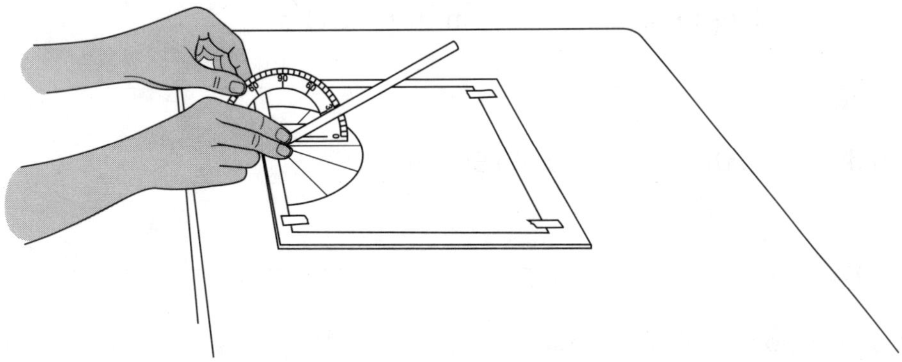

▲ **Figure 4** Adjust the straw's tilt to match your community's latitude.

☐ 9. **OBSERVE:** Check the time. When the clock reads on the hour, such as 10:00 A.M., observe the shadow of the straw. Use a pencil to mark the position of the shadow. Label the mark *1*. Record the time, date, and observations for mark *1* in Table 1.

☐ 10. Return to your sundial every hour on the hour throughout the day. Mark and number each position of the straw's shadow and record the times, dates, and observations in Table 1. You may wish to record the hourly shadow positions for several consecutive days.

OBSERVATIONS

Table 1: Tracking the Sun's Motion

Clock Time	Mark #	Observations
1		
2		
3		
4		
5		
6		
7		
8		

1. **OBSERVE:** About how many degrees does the Sun's shadow move each hour?

2. **COMPARE:** At which numbered mark is the shadow of the Sun at its highest point?

3. What is the clock time that corresponds with this mark?

CONCLUSIONS

4. **COMPARE:** The shadow of the Sun will be at its highest point at noon solar time. At your location, how does noon solar time compare with noon clock time?

5. **INFER:** Why do you think that solar time and clock time are not exactly the same?

6. **ANALYZE:** Can you accurately measure the passage of hours, using solar time? Explain.

Name ______________________ Class ______________ Date ______________

LABORATORY CHALLENGE FOR LESSON 2-7

How does a heat shield work?

Materials

- safety goggles
- lab apron
- scissors
- aluminum foil
- metric ruler
- 2 large paper cups
- felt-tip pen
- paper towels
- masking tape
- water
- 2 heat sources
- 2 ring stands with clamps
- 2 thermometers
- clock or watch with second hand
- 2 burette clamps

BACKGROUND: In a space vehicle like the space shuttle, insulation in the form of a heat shield is needed to protect both the vehicle and the astronauts from extremely high temperatures when the space vehicle reenters Earth's atmosphere. The space shuttle uses ceramic tiles that can withstand temperatures of nearly 3,000°F.

PURPOSE: In this challenge, you will demonstrate how a heat shield works.

PROCEDURE

❑ **1.** Put on safety goggles and a lab apron.

❑ **2.** Cut 5 pieces of aluminum foil, each approximately 30 cm × 30 cm. Cover the outside of a paper cup with one piece of aluminum foil. Using a felt-tip pen, label this cup *A* and set it aside.

❑ **3.** Cover the outside of a second paper cup with a piece of paper towel. Mold the paper towel to fit the shape of the cup and fold it over the top edge of the cup, as shown in Figure 1.

❑ **4.** Over the paper towel on the second cup, place two layers of aluminum foil. Mold the foil to the shape of the cup. Then, wrap another layer of paper towel over the foil.

❑ **5.** Cover this second layer of paper towel with two more layers of aluminum foil. Mold the foil to the shape of the cup. If necessary, tape the foil in place at the top edge of the cup. Label this cup *B*.

❑ **6.** Fill each cup about three-quarters full of water. Set each cup on a heat source.

❑ **7.** Use clamps to attach each of two thermometers to its own ring stand. ⚠ **CAUTION: Handle thermometers carefully.** Position the ring stands so that the thermometer bulbs are in the water inside each cup, as shown in Figure 2 on the next page. Do not let the thermometer touch the sides or bottom of the cups.

❑ **8.** **MEASURE:** Read the thermometer in each cup. Record the temperatures in Table 1 on page 20 under "0 min."

❑ **9.** Turn on the heat sources and carefully heat the water in the cups. ⚠ **CAUTION: Observe all safety rules when using a heat source.**

❑ **10.** **MEASURE:** After 1 min, turn off the heat sources and record the temperature of the water in each cup. Record your measurements in Table 1.

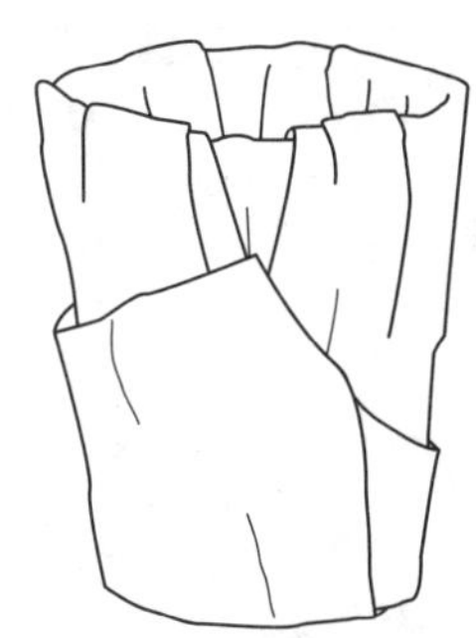

▲ **Figure 1** Wrap a cup in a paper towel.

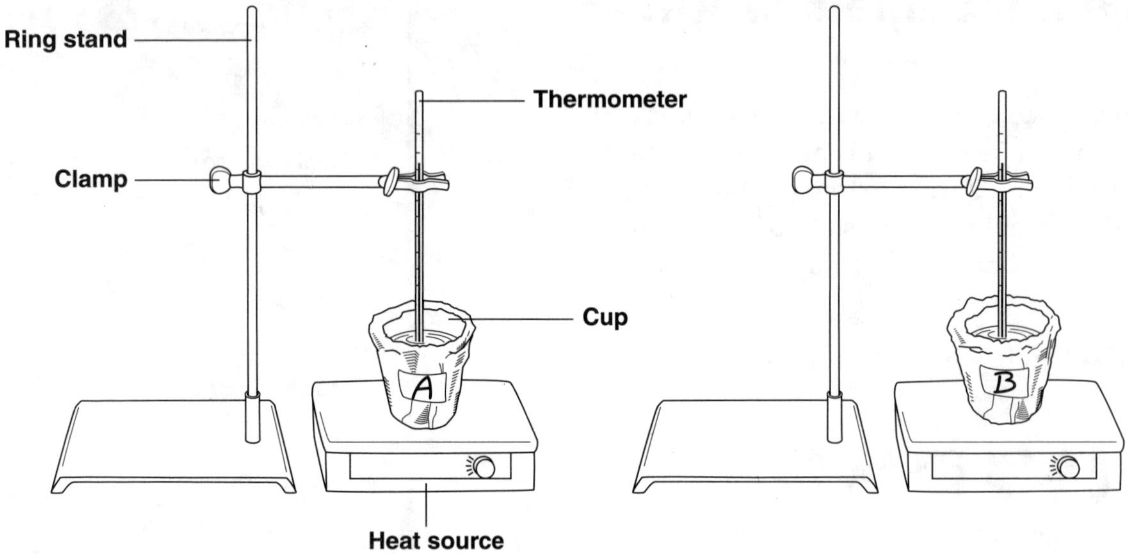

▲ **Figure 2** Attach the thermometers to the ring stands.

OBSERVATIONS

Table 1: Observing a Heat Shield		
	Temperature (°C)	
Cup	0 min	1 min
A		
B		

1. **OBSERVE:** How much did the temperature of the water increase in cup A? ___________

2. **OBSERVE:** How much did the temperature of the water increase in cup B? ___________

CONCLUSIONS

3. **RELATE:** In which cup was the water protected from heat outside the cup? ___________

4. **INFER:** In this investigation, what materials served as a heat shield?

____

5. **COMPARE:** How is the cup's heat shield similar to a space shuttle's heat shield?

____

____

____

Name ______________________ Class ______________ Date ______________

LABORATORY CHALLENGE FOR LESSON 3-1

How can a scale model of the solar system be made?

Materials

- pencil
- string
- meter stick
- scissors
- 2 sheets of paper (about 1.5 m × 1.5 m)
- drawing compass

BACKGROUND: A scale model shows relative sizes of objects. A scale model also can show the relative distances among objects. Can you make a scale model of the planets that shows both their relative diameters and their relative distances from the Sun?

PURPOSE: In this activity, you will compare the sizes of the planets and their distances from the Sun. You also will discover some of the problems that result when trying to make a scale model of the solar system.

PROCEDURE

❑ **1.** Look at Table 1 on page 23. Using the scale 1 cm = 10,000 km, calculate the scale diameter of the Sun. You can find the scale diameter easily by moving the decimal point in the actual measurement four places to the left.

diameter of the Sun = 1,392,000 km

scale diameter = 139.2 cm

Write the scale diameter of the Sun in Table 1.

❑ **2. CALCULATE:** Using the scale 1 cm = 10,000 km, calculate the scale diameter for each planet. Round your answers to the nearest 0.1 cm. Write these measurements in Table 1.

❑ **3. CALCULATE:** Using the scale 1 cm = 10,000 km, calculate the scale distance from the Sun for each planet. Round your answers to the nearest 100 cm. Write these measurements in Table 1.

❑ **4.** Tie a pencil to one end of a piece of string. Starting at the pencil, measure and cut the string so that its length is one-half of the scale diameter of the Sun. This is the scale radius of the Sun.

❑ 5. **MODEL:** As shown in Figure 1, use the pencil and string like a compass to draw a circle equal in diameter to the scale diameter of the Sun. (Remember that the radius of a circle is equal to half its diameter.) To make the circle, have a lab partner hold the end of the string down in the center of one of the sheets of paper. This will be the center of the circle that represents the Sun.

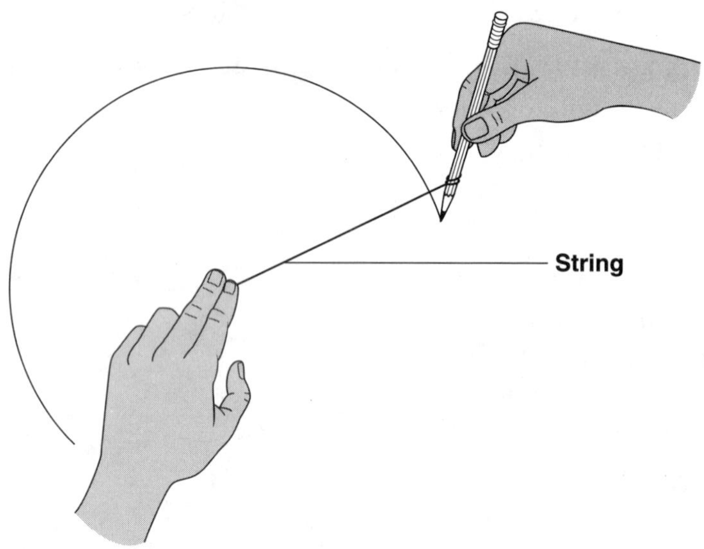

▲ **Figure 1** Draw a circle that represents the Sun.

❑ 6. Stretch the string out taut over the paper. Hold the pencil vertically with its point touching the paper. While you trace the circle, your partner should hold down the string, turning the fingers so that they point to and move with the pencil.

❑ 7. Use scissors to cut out the circle. ⚠ **CAUTION: Always be careful when using scissors.** Label the circle *Sun.*

❑ 8. Repeat Steps 4–7 for each planet, using a drawing compass to draw your circles. Label each circle with the name of the planet it represents.

LABORATORY CHALLENGE FOR LESSON 3-1 *(continued)*

OBSERVATIONS

Table 1: Dimensions of Solar System

Sun/Planet	Diameter (km)	Scale Diameter (cm)	Average Distance From Sun (km)	Scale Distance (cm)
Sun	1,392,000	139.2	———	———
Mercury	4,878		57,000,000	
Venus	12,104		108,000,000	
Earth	12,756		150,000,000	
Mars	6,794		228,000,000	
Jupiter	143,884		778,000,000	
Saturn	120,536		1,427,000,000	
Uranus	51,118		2,870,000,000	
Neptune	50,538		4,497,000,000	
Pluto	2,324		5,900,000,000	

1. **COMPARE:** How does the diameter of the largest planet compare with the diameter of the Sun?

____

____

2. **COMPARE:** How does the diameter of the smallest planet compare with the diameter of the largest planet?

____

____

3. **CALCULATE:** Look at the scale distance of Mercury from the Sun. Express this distance in meters.

____

4. What is the scale distance of Pluto from the Sun? Express this distance in meters.

____

CONCLUSIONS

5. **ANALYZE:** Can you construct a model of the solar system that uses scale models of the planets to compare their sizes? Explain.

____

6. **ANALYZE:** Can you construct a scale model of the solar system that shows accurately the relative distances of the planets from the Sun as well as the sizes of the planets? Why or why not?

____

____

____

____

CRITICAL THINKING

7. **ANALYZE:** To construct the scale model described in question 6, would it help to use a different scale, such as 1 cm = 1 million km? Explain.

____

____

Name ______________________ Class ______________ Date ______________

LABORATORY CHALLENGE FOR LESSON 4-2

How can light from stars be studied?

Materials

- diffraction grating
- assorted colored pencils or markers
- incandescent lamp
- fluorescent lamp
- gas vapor tubes (sodium, neon, hydrogen)

BACKGROUND: When white light passes through a diffraction grating, it is broken up into the colors of the visible spectrum. When a body such as a star gives off light, the colors in the light's spectrum vary according to the elements that are present in the star. This happens because the light given off by each element has a characteristic wavelength. Each wavelength produces a different color. If a certain color is missing from a star's spectrum, you know that the corresponding element is not present in the star.

PURPOSE: In this activity, you will use a diffraction grating to observe light from different sources. You will also see how elements can be identified by their spectra.

PROCEDURE

❑ **1.** Hold up a diffraction grating and look at a bright part of the sky. **⚠ CAUTION: Never look directly at the Sun.**

❑ **2.** **OBSERVE:** Move the diffraction grating in front of your eyes until you see a spectrum form on the grating. Use colored pencils or markers to make a drawing of this spectrum in the space labeled Diagram 1.

▲ **Diagram 1** Spectrum: light from sky

❑ **3.** **OBSERVE:** Turn on an incandescent lamp. Hold the diffraction grating in front of the lamp, as shown in Figure 1, and observe the spectrum. Draw the spectrum in the space labeled Diagram 2. Turn off the lamp.

▲ **Figure 1** Observe the spectrum produced by light from an incandescent lamp.

▲ **Diagram 2** Spectrum: incandescent lamp

❑ **4. OBSERVE:** Turn on a fluorescent lamp. Observe the light through the diffraction grating. Make a drawing of what you see in the space labeled Diagram 3. Turn off the lamp.

▲ **Diagram 3** Spectrum: fluorescent lamp

❑ **5. OBSERVE:** Look through the diffraction grating at a lighted sodium vapor tube, as shown in Figure 2. In the space labeled Diagram 4, draw the spectrum that you see.

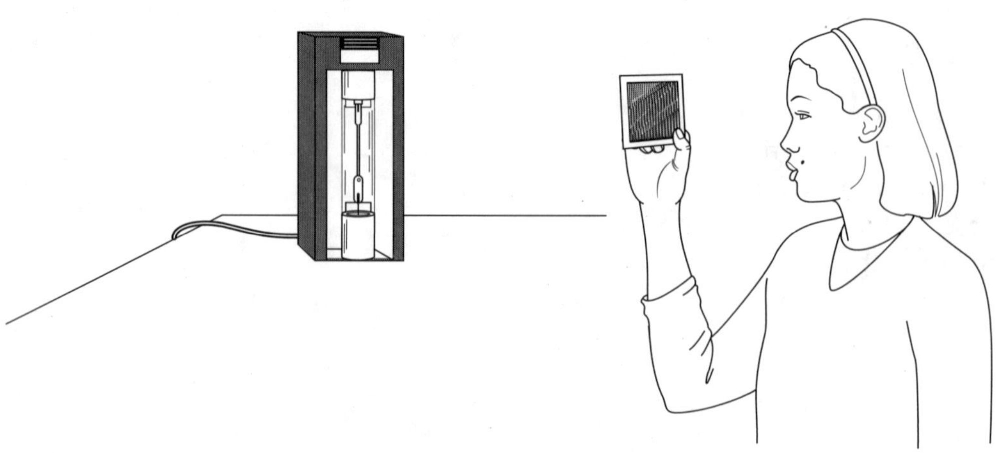

▲ **Figure 2** Observe the spectrum produced by light from a sodium vapor tube.

▲ **Diagram 4** Spectrum: sodium

❑ 6. **OBSERVE:** Look through the diffraction grating at a lighted neon vapor tube. In the space labeled Diagram 5, draw the spectrum that you see.

▲ **Diagram 5** Spectrum: neon

❑ 7. **OBSERVE:** Look through the diffraction grating at a lighted hydrogen vapor tube. In the space labeled Diagram 6, draw the spectrum that you see.

▲ **Diagram 6** Spectrum: hydrogen

OBSERVATIONS

1. **OBSERVE:** What does a diffraction grating do to light? ______

2. **COMPARE:** How does the spectrum from an incandescent lamp compare with the spectrum of natural light?

______

3. **CONTRAST:** How is the spectrum from a fluorescent lamp different from the spectrum from an incandescent lamp?

______

4. **CONTRAST:** How are spectra from the sodium, neon, and hydrogen vapor tubes different from the spectra from the lamps?

______

CONCLUSIONS

5. **ANALYZE:** What is the characteristic spectrum for the element sodium? ______

6. **ANALYZE:** What is the characteristic spectrum for the element neon? ______

7. **ANALYZE:** What is the characteristic spectrum for the element hydrogen? ______

8. **ANALYZE:** What information can a diffraction grating give about a star? ______